RANTINGS
OF A
BITTER CHILDLESS
WOMAN

THE PARENTING BOOK'S
EVIL TWIN

BY JEANNE BELLEZZO

WriteIdeas

Before We Get Started

I'm really not a bitter childless woman. I'm a woman, and I have no children. No reason, really. I never made a conscious decision not to have kids — it just never happened. Thank God I didn't have them with my ex-husband (despite his argument that having kids would "fix" our marriage, although probably not his incessant lying and narcissism issues) and I haven't remarried. I like kids, but having them as a single mom isn't a good option for me. I am, however, a fun "aunt" to several of my friends' children, and I enjoy spending time with them and seeing them grow up. (One even gives me surfing tips.)

The "bitter" part? That really only applies to parents who think their kids are more important than anyone else, can do no wrong, and expect everyone to accept their behavior. And that's when the ranting begins…

I know from experience that some readers will take umbrage. They'll say, "Well obviously she just has no idea what it's like to be a parent." And they are absolutely right, which I make clear in many rants. Only people with kids understand what it's like to be a parent. But on the flip side, only people without kids know what it's like to not be a parent in a society where reproducing is the norm. As a friend once put it, "It never even occurred to me not to have kids." In a world of mommy blogs and parenting books, mine is simply a different perspective.

And since it's inevitably going to come up, yes, I do have cats. Two. What kind of credibility would I have for this book without them? I do not, however, have cat pillows, cat blankets, cat art, cat t-shirts, cat towels or cat mugs (ok, one, but it was a gift), and I am not a crazy cat lady. Yet.

I hope you enjoy my book. And please visit *Rantings of a Bitter Childless Woman* on Facebook to share your own stories.

Thank you! (By the way, there's a rant about that.)

I have no idea what it is like to have kids.

Table Contents

Before We Get Started

Teachable Moments

Planes, Trains & Automobiles

Happy Holidays

Reproductive Rights. And Wrongs

Parents Behaving Badly

It Takes a Village of Idiots

Elsewhere in the Village

Teachable Moments

To Hear This Message in Toddler, Press 3

I don't speak toddler. I've tried, I really have, and it just isn't in my vocabulary. I can't have coherent conversations with drunk people when I'm sober, and that's how I feel when I talk to a toddler.

So when my friends allow (or worse yet, encourage) their toddlers to answer the phone — regardless of the fact that they can barely string a noun and verb together — I know it's going to be a painful interaction. Exhibit A (names have been changed to protect my friendships):

Ring, ring. Fumbling with phone. Phone is dropped and loudly strikes furniture. Shuffling noises. And finally:

1

"Hewo?"

"Hi Kennedy! Is mommy there?"

"Hewo?"

"Hi honey, put mommy on the phone, ok?"

"Mommy?"

"No, Kennedy, I need you to go get mommy please."

"I made poop."

What does one say in response to this? I don't even know if that's a good thing or a bad thing in this case — but I'm not about to ask for clarification. Either way, it's not why I'm calling.

"Ok...um, go get mommy, ok?"

"K." Phone is again dropped and call is promptly disconnected.

In our carefree college days when none of us could even imagine being parents, my friends and I all swore we would never put our children on the phone or, especially, allow them to leave a message on voice mail. But one by one, they crossed over to the dark side, permitting their toddlers to record an outgoing message while they "coached" them through it. So when my call goes to voice mail, it sounds like this:

Kid: "Hi."

Mom in background: "Say, 'We're not here to take your call right now.'"

Kid: "We're not...what?"

Mom: "Not here right now."

Kid: "Hi not here right now."

Mom: "Say, 'Please leave a message and we'll call you back.'"

Kid: "Please...what?"

Mom: "Leave a message."

Kid: "Leave a message."

Mom: "And we'll call you back."

Kid: "And we'll call you back."

Mom: "Now say, 'Thank you for calling.'"

Kid: "What?"

By now I've forgotten why I called and I feel like I'm at a parrot convention.

I'm betting whoever invented texting had a lot of friends with toddlers.

PAPER OR PLASTIC?

I was at the grocery store, waiting in line behind a mom and her son, who was probably somewhere between ages three and eight. (One of the things about not having kids is being really bad at estimating age.) There were several people behind me in line, and the mom was holding out a handful of change while her son tried to count out 32 cents for the cashier. Which could have been cute if the kid had the slightest clue what he was doing.

"Give the nice lady three dimes and two pennies. No, honey, that's not a dime. That's a nickel. The dimes are the small ones, remember? Good. Now two more dimes. No, just two more. And now two pennies. Remember which one is the penny? " And on and on, while the rest of us in line looked on with tight-lipped smiles. Mom proudly informed the cashier, who displayed infinite patience and grace, "He just loves to count out money."

I'm all for teachable moments — in the right place, at the right time. But while you're teaching your son to count change, how about teaching him Consideration for Other People's Time or This Is How You Swipe the Credit Card?

Better yet, teach him to use the self-checkout lanes. He'll never want to go shopping again.

THE MAGIC WORD

As a non-parent, I take pains to avoid committing the mortal sin that is disciplining other people's children. Unless someone's about to lose an eye, I keep my mouth shut.

But I'm tempted to draw the line at basic manners. Seriously, when did kids stop saying please and thank you? And when did their parents stop making a big deal — or even blinking an eye — when their offspring demonstrate a complete lack of manners?

Case in point: I recently attended a neighborhood get-together at a friend's house. One of the guests, a woman I'd never met before who clearly just missed the cut for Real Housewives of Orange County, dumped her four gorgeous young children at the pool and proceeded to park herself across the yard with a drink in her hand and her back to the pool. Apparently she expected the rest of us to make sure her kids didn't drown.

Shortly thereafter — I wasn't there for this incident, but hearsay is admissible in rants — the 11-year-old strolled into the kitchen, put one hand on her hip and tossed her hair in a flawless imitation of Paris Hilton, and demanded, "Chips."

That was it. "Chips."

Not, "Excuse me, may I have some chips?" Or, "Could we please have some chips?" or even, "Chips, please. And be quick about it."

No. Just "Chips."

Looks were exchanged among the adults, and then someone handed her a bag of chips. She smiled and thanked them profusely. Ha! I'm joking. Future trophy wife took the bag without a word and walked back out to the pool.

Less than an hour later, her younger sister tapped me on the shoulder and said, "I want cranberry juice." I suggested she ask her mom. She looked at me as if I had recommended she grow another head, and then uncertainly wandered off to find her mom. (Which wasn't hard, because mom hadn't moved from where she'd been holding court since she arrived.) I don't know if she ever got the juice.

Perhaps because her children are absolutely beautiful, she feels there's no need for them to be polite. I later learned that her twins had been on a sitcom and were used to having things done for them. Ohhhhhh...okay then.

But it's not just these kids. An eight-year-old son of a friend once instructed me to hand over mustard at a birthday party. I believe his exact words were, "Gimme the mustard." I asked — as playfully as I could muster knowing I might be crossing the volatile don't-discipline-my-kid line — "What's the magic word?" In response, he rolled his eyes as if he couldn't believe I was going to force him to be polite and muttered, "Please."

(For the record, I've been known to ask adults for the magic word as well. Honestly, it's kind of fun to see their reaction.)

My good friend Mary, who has four kids but has been known to forget and say she has five, has noticed a disturbing trend among kids not with "please" but "thank you." Instead of saying "No, thank you" when she offers them something, they say, "I'm good" or sometimes even, "Meh."

"Every time I hear it, it makes me bristle," she said. "I wasn't asking how you are. I was generously offering you something which merits a proper 'no, thank you.'"

Since she pointed this out, I've noticed it not only with kids, but adults as well.

"Do you want a beer?"

"Nah, I'm good."

Don't you learn "please" and "thank you" at an early age? Kindergarten? Preschool? Sesame Street? Am I being unreasonable to expect someone who is 8 — or 12 or 50 — to practice Manners 101? It's respect, pure and simple, and it seems to be endangered.

So please, teach your kids some manners and set a good example yourself. And thank you for reading.

LET'S PRETEND!

Several years ago, an air traffic controller allowed his child to direct airplanes at a major New York airport. As my friend Nancy put it, "I guess now there will be an abrupt halt to Bring Your Child to Work Day at JFK."

And while I can see where a child would get a huge thrill out of playing air traffic controller, did it ever occur to the people in the tower that the microphone really didn't need to be on?

Here's a nutty idea — pretend! It's ok to pretend with children! (In fact, let them do it while they can, because once they're out of, say, college, pretending doesn't go over so well in the real world.)

For example, maybe pretend your son is walking your huge dog all by himself, but be prepared to grab the leash if someone approaches. That way, when I run past you on the boardwalk and your dog takes off after me, your poor terrified child won't get dragged helplessly behind and burst into tears. (And somehow, judging by the stinkeye mom gives me, this is my fault.)

Or, maybe pretend your daughter is leaving the outgoing message on your voice mail, instead of really letting her do it? So that callers aren't subjected to three excruciating minutes of your toddler trying to record a comprehensible message? Can I put my cat on my answering machine? The end result will sound pretty much the same.

Good thing I can pretend it's cute.

When I was growing up there was no "she's just a kid" excuse when I misbehaved.

There was "you do that again and I'll knock you into next week!"

PLANES, TRAINS &
AUTOMOBILES

OH PLEASE

When I was little, if my mom wanted me to stop doing something, she'd say, "Stop doing that." Usually, the activity ceased almost immediately. If not, she'd say it again, a little more sternly. If that didn't work, there were consequences.

So I'm wondering when firm parental direction regarding bad behavior gave way to polite, meek requests. Case in point: Lucas and his mom, sitting behind me on the airplane. We hadn't even taken off, and Lucas was kicking the back of my seat.

Mom took action. Sort of.

"Lucas, please don't kick the seat."

Kicking stops. For a few minutes.

"I asked you to stop kicking that lady's seat."

Kicking resumes.

"Lucas, I'm asking you. Please don't kick the seat. That isn't nice for the person sitting there."

Soccer practice continues. At which point "the lady" turns around and says to Lucas (who is really very cute), "Honey, please don't kick my seat."

"I've asked him to stop," Mom says apologetically.

The lady, already terrified that she has crossed the "don't discipline my kid" line, forces a smile and successfully contains the urge to suggest that mom actually TELL HER CHILD TO STOP KICKING MY SEAT. And perhaps physically restrain him from doing so?

Please?

A 2013 survey conducted on behalf of Expedia's 2013 Airplane Etiquette Study asked 1,001 adult travelers how they feel about certain in-flight behaviors. Here are a few results:

- "Inattentive Parents" (41%) and "Rear Seat Kickers" (38%) ranked first and second on the list of "Most Annoying / Offensive Airplane Etiquette Violators"

- 63 percent of those polled admitted they're often annoyed by parents traveling with loud children

- 49 percent would pay extra to be seated in a child-free area (59 percent of this group included Americans aged 34 and under)

And a Facebook group called "Airlines Should Have Kid Free Flights!" counts more than 1,000 members to date.

Jet Set Betty, a flight attendant for 16 years with two major U.S. airlines, blogs about life on board.

Jet Set Betty described an incident with the parent of a very active toddler. Children under age two are not required to have a purchased seat; instead, parents can hold the children on their laps during the flight. When the seatbelt sign is on, parents are required to fasten their belt and hold their child.

This particular parent would not hold onto her child despite Jet Set Betty's repeated requests. At one point, Betty gently explained that she was the mother of three and knew how difficult traveling with a child could be. Rather than corral her child, the mother angrily said that her daughter would scream and cry if she had to sit still. The mother then began screaming at Betty, accusing her of making it "the worst flight ever" and saying that she never wanted to travel again.

CARPOOLISHNESS

I live in Southern California, which means it generally takes three times as long to drive someplace as it does anywhere else in the country. I bought my first car shortly after I moved here almost 20 years ago from Chicago, where a car is more of a nuisance than a necessity. Seeing as how San Diego is a mecca for runners, cyclists, surfers, swimmers and many other physical activities, I was surprised to find that very few people walk anywhere (unless they're walking for exercise). As a result, we have lots of traffic. And as a result of that, we have carpool lanes. And as a result of that, I'm annoyed.

Here's how it works: In order to receive the California Highway Patrol's blessing to use these sacred pathways, you must have more than one person in your vehicle (or pay extra for a special pass, but let's not even go there). Multiple occupants should mean fewer cars on the road, more efficient travel, lower emissions, yada, yada. So far, so good.

However, that means mom and her three kids – none of whom are old enough to operate a Big Wheel, much less a motor vehicle – can use the carpool lane while I sit fuming in traffic. So can dad and his infant in the car seat, or mom taking the sixth-grade girls to soccer. These vehicles, like mine, have just one licensed driver. But they're allowed to speed merrily ahead of the rest of us.

So by the same token, shouldn't I be able to use the carpool lane when I take my cat to the vet? He has about as much right and ability to drive as the 8-year-old carpooler drawing on the back of his mom's seat with a Sharpie and making faces at us unwashed masses in the lowly regular lanes.

There was actually a case of a pregnant woman who went to court after being ticketed for using the carpool lane. She claimed her fetus counted as a person. Given the current carpool rules, I actually agreed with her. And so did the judge.

My point is this: Carpool lanes should be restricted to two or more licensed drivers. And no, I don't expect CHP to stop every mom and her teenagers to verify their ages. But when it's a mom and a baby, or dad picking up junior from preschool, isn't it kind of obvious?

My mom friends to whom I have subjected this

rant agree with me in principle, but they're not about to give up the privilege of cruising in the carpool lane while the rest of us crawl along at a snail's pace. As one put it: "Anyone who's ever had a kid who has to go to the bathroom knows why moms need to use those lanes!" (Because we adults never have the same conundrum?)

Fortunately, I don't drive that often. And when I do, I guess I'll just sit patiently in traffic and catch up on texting.

(Mom, I'm kidding.)

PARKING FOR THE UNBORN

I f you've been in a car with me, you probably know that I have a Parking Guardian Angel. She ensures that I get a prime parking spot even in the most crowded, popular or parking-challenged destinations. She usually appears as soon as one of my passengers says, "We'll never get a spot." Like magic, one opens up just ahead. (Of course, if I had a choice, I'd prefer a Lottery Guardian Angel. But I'll take what I can get.)

Recently, though, we encountered a parking scenario that may cause her to hang up her wings. I'm talking about parking spots reserved for kids — specifically, kids who haven't even been born yet. "Expectant Mother Parking": four primo spots at the mall, reserved exclusively for pregnant women.

When I first spotted the empty spaces just steps

from the main walkway, I thought my Parking Guardian Angel had outdone herself. She probably thought so too – until we saw the pink parking stripes and cute little pink sign sweetly informing us that unless I was with child I should just keep driving. Not knocked up? Don't even think about parking here, sister.

First young kids, including babies, were allowed to commandeer the carpool lanes. Now the unborn have priority parking.

And of course, three of the four spots were open. Because really, how much reserved pregnant parking does one mall actually need on any given day?

I was tempted to park there anyway. After all, I *could* be pregnant. Highly unlikely, but technically not impossible. And really, is anyone going to ask me to prove it? Are the parking police lined up with Clearblue® pregnancy tests, ready to corral me to the restroom and validate my reproductive status?

If pregnant women merit their own parking spots because of the potential physical discomfort brought on by either acts of their own volition or their failure to ensure adequate prevention, how about some premier parking for those of us with killer, Satan-is-in-my-uterus-with-a-crowbar menstrual cramps as a result of NOT being pregnant? Why do we have to limp across the parking lot doubled over in pain on our way to get Midol while mommies-to-be practically get valet service?

And what about post-partum moms who have to schlep around the newborn, stroller, and countless accoutrements of new motherhood? Isn't their need for a convenient spot even greater than a pregnant woman's? (Yes, if "New Mom Parking" existed, I'd rant about that. But I'm just making a point here).

After I debated whether I might have valid grounds for a discrimination lawsuit, I drove away. I could feel a major headache coming on, and I didn't feel like shopping anymore.

Unless there was "People with a Headache Parking."

Fear of Flying

I'm not a big fan of flying. It's usually a major hassle, overcrowded and generally uncomfortable. Every time I fly, I wonder how the flight attendants manage to keep smiling, repeat safety instructions countless times and not strangle several people.

Like the woman who was clearly preparing to change her baby's diaper in the seat when the passing flight attendant sweetly asked her, "Do you know where the changing table is in the back?" The woman confirmed that she did. Five minutes later, when she spotted the naked baby being changed on the seat, the flight attendant added tersely, "Meaning, *don't change your baby on the seat.*"

Or like the gentleman in front of me, who rang for the flight attendant midway through our flight. When she arrived, he offered her a plastic beverage cup filled to the brim. With urine. "He had to go," dad explained. His son was at least five years old, so I'm thinking there was a good chance he was toilet-trained. But as we all know, I'm not a parent.

The horrified flight attendant backed away as if he had held out a, well, cup full of fresh urine. "Sir, we're not allowed to take that," she said, valiantly trying to disguise her disgust but failing miserably. "You need to take that to the restroom and empty it."

He seemed genuinely surprised — and a little peeved — that the flight attendant was not eager to collect his son's bodily fluids. Perplexed, he glanced back toward the bathroom. Then he said something to his wife, who placed a paper cocktail napkin over the top of the cup. Nervously holding the cup at arm's length in front of him, he tried to rush down the narrow aisle without spilling. Remember that birthday party game we played as kids where we'd each balance a raw egg on a spoon and race for the finish line without dropping it? It was just like that. But with urine.

My sister, who was waiting in line to use the bathroom (something this gentleman and his son apparently were not familiar with), said he went directly to the front of the line and ran into the next available room, splashing urine the entire time. Moments later, the flight attendant made a mad dash behind him with latex gloves, a cloth and a spray bottle clearly marked "biohazard."

I think this may be how skydiving got started.

Dying of Boredom

Remember when we took long car trips as kids and amused ourselves for hours on end by playing The Alphabet Game? You know, where you had to point out an object starting with each consecutive letter of the alphabet before your bratty sister could? And if you both spotted the same object simultaneously, you fought about it, thus passing another 15 to 20 minutes of the trip until your dad finally warned you not to make him stop this car and turn around right now?

Life was so simple then.

Now, kids on long car trips (defined as 10 minutes or more) have a plethora of entertainment options we couldn't even imagine. DVD players. Cell phones. Nintendo DS. Online shopping. Mobile investing. Personally, I think it would have been the coolest thing in the world to have movies in the back of our old Wrangler and then fight with my sister about what to watch. But apparently, it isn't enough for today's short-attention-span generation. Barely an hour into an 8-hour family roadtrip to Arizona, my friend's six-year-old son turned off the DVD player, tossed his DS impatiently into his pile of books, and announced, "I'm bored."

A few months ago, my boyfriend and I volunteered to watch his twin niece and nephew while mom and dad went to a baseball game with friends from out of town. They dropped the kids off early on Sunday morning. (For us, any time before 8 a.m. on Sunday is early. Thank God for coffee.)

We spent the next few hours playing games with them (side note: if you're ever having issues waking up, a few games of Jenga will resolve them immediately). We watched cartoons. They chased the cats around. We took them to lunch (the kids, not the cats). We took them to a movie, stopping first to get something to drink at the grocery store, and while we were there we bought them each a doughnut. Yes, they just had lunch, but as the fun aunt and uncle we are required by law to overdose them on sugar. And they're both thin little Energizer bunnies, so we weren't particularly concerned about childhood obesity.

As they wolfed down their fried sugary goodness, one mentioned that it was the second doughnut she'd had. I asked, "Today?" She replied, "No, ever. Mom doesn't let us have doughnuts." Awesome. This will be our little secret, right?

So after games, cartoons, lunch, clandestine doughnuts, and a movie, we returned home and made a beeline for the couch, exhausted. (Ok, the adults were exhausted. Seriously parents, *how* do you do it?)

At which point one of the twins asked, "Can we do something fun now?"

Yes. Go outside and play The Alphabet Game. Twice.

(By the way, they told on us about the doughnuts.)

Happy Holidays

Trick or Treat or Else

The older I get, the scarier Halloween becomes. Let's start with the costumes. While the witches, ghosts, vampires and monsters are pretend-scary, the cost of some of these getups is genuinely terrifying. When did kids stop competing for the best collection of candy, and start competing for the most outrageously priced costume? One of my friends paid $90 for her 10-year-old daughter's Disney-character attire. (I don't know which character. I don't have kids, which is why I'm here in the first place.) And of course, the night before, the girl decided she'd rather be an '80s girl and used her own clothes to make a costume.

Which, I might point out, was what we always did as kids. When I was your age, missy, we made our own costumes from things we found around the house: random scraps from mom's sewing kit for pirate eye patches, pipe cleaners for whiskers and antennae, burned corks for black eyes and dirt, feathers for Indian headdresses, and bandannas on sticks for hobos.

Of course, kids today can't be Indians. Or hobos (sorry, "transients"). Or any other costume that used to be harmless and fun but is now politically incorrect and shockingly unacceptable. It's hard to find a costume these days that doesn't offend someone. Gypsy? Offensive to Gypsies. Indian squaw? Offensive to Native Americans. Bullfighter? Offensive to Latinos and bulls. Skeleton? Offensive to supermodels. And so on.

(And while we're on the subject, have you ever noticed how many men dress up as women every Halloween? A male friend admitted to me that he was curious to know what it was like to have "boobs." Really.)

Anyway, when I was a kid, we also actually sang "Trick or Treat!" with enthusiasm when someone came to the door. Apparently, some kids now can't be bothered. They just hold out the bag, collect the candy, and walk away without so much as a "Thank you."

When did Halloween become a National Day of Entitlement?

By the way, if you're:

a) sporting a beard, facial piercings or tattoos that aren't fake;

b) out alone past dark; and/or

c) taller than me

then you're too old to be trick or treating. But since I'm not sure if your gangsta attire (offensive to much of East LA, incidentally) is a costume or not, take all the mini-Snickers you want.

Halloween Hotties

Forget the high-tech haunted houses and I-think-this-might-actually-be-real fake blood. The most terrifying part of Halloween? The blatantly sexy costumes designed for pre-teen girls.

When I was a kid, Halloween meant dressing up as a hobo, Gypsy, or Indian squaw. I guess because these costumes are now considered politically incorrect (in fact, some schools have replaced any mention of Halloween at all with the generic term "Fall Festival"), girls now have only one option: slutty.

An online search of girls' costumes produces truly frightening results. The Little Red Riding Hood costume comes "complete with fishnet stockings." I'm pretty sure the original Ms. Hood was not navigating the dark woods in fishnets.

Snow White now wears a bustier. The dwarfs

would be horrified. (Well, maybe not Happy. Nothing seems to bother him.)

Gothic Angel has "a dangerously intriguing look." Just what you want for your sweet little girl.

Geisha Girl. (Indian squaw is offensive, but Japanese prostitute is perfectly acceptable?)

Vampire. Warrior Princess. Policewoman. Sassy Devil. All sexed up. (And no, adding "Sassy" to the description does not make it okay.)

The scariest part? Many of these are "For ages 4 and up."

Don't let your 3-year-old get her hands on it, though. The label clearly states: "WARNING: CHOKING HAZARD – Small Parts. Not for children under 3 years."

EAT, DRINK AND GO SHOPPING

What happened to Thanksgiving? We used to have Halloween, then Thanksgiving, then Christmas/Hannukah/Kwaanza/ Festivus. (For simplicity, I'm referring to the December holiday as Christmas. Feel free to substitute your own holiday.)

Anyway. With every passing year, Christmas paraphernalia creeps in earlier. And earlier. First it was right after Thanksgiving, then right before, then early November. Now Thanksgiving is ignored altogether. Overnight, ghoulish masks morph into Santa's smiling mug. Like a kaleidoscope, orange and black suddenly change to red and green. On the night of October 31, kids are collecting candy from costumed store owners along our main street. By the next morning, those stores are fully decked out with ornaments, wreaths and carols.

My friend went shopping for Thanksgiving table decorations several days later, and the saleslady told her, in a tone clearly reserved for toddlers, non-native English speakers and morons, "Oh, honey, we don't have Thanksgiving items any more. We cleared them all out before Halloween."

Did I miss something? Didn't we used to care about Thanksgiving? Didn't it mean something besides the eve of Black Friday and the official start of the holiday shopping madness?

Wait for it....

You don't shop for Thanksgiving. There are no extravagant gifts or pricey costumes or hoarding of enough candy and cookies to rot even Kanye West's diamond-studded teeth. There's the problem. Thanksgiving isn't about buying as much stuff as we possibly can—it's about being thankful for what we already have. Especially things money can't buy, like family and good friends and health.

No wonder retailers aren't interested. Unless they sell turkey and maybe some green beans and pumpkin pies, what's in it for them?

We can only hope the schools are still teaching kids about Thanksgiving, and having them put on plays about pilgrims and Indians, and creating turkeys out of paper plates and construction paper. They need to know that there's more to Thanksgiving than just two whole days off school. Let's all remember the true meaning of this day: Gathering together with family and friends, eating enough to sustain a small country, and then piling into the car at midnight and being the first in line when Walmart opens at 3 a.m.

HOLIDAY STUFF-ING

America's most revered holiday — Black Friday — is just days away, and families across the country are gearing up for the season of giving. Actually, make that "give me." A full 10 days before Thanksgiving, two women in San Diego got in line outside a Best Buy to ensure they would be first in to snag the big fancy loss-leader TV on Black Friday. The news showed pictures of them literally camped out (complete with a tent) in front of the store, sitting in umbrella chairs with a cooler and a double wide tin of Pringles between them. Apparently it's important to keep your strength up when you're sitting around for over a week waiting for a store to open. (And I'm sorry, but these women already clearly spend way too much time in front of their current television sets.) When the security guard asked them to move, they did. To another Best Buy.

Who has this much free time? Do they work? And if not, how can they afford a huge new flat screen TV?

And more importantly, where are their kids?

I know, foolish question. Their kids are no doubt wishfully texting Santa with copious holiday gift demands, er, requests that defy our shaky economy.

My friend's daughter recently showed me her dream gift in the American Girl® catalog: An American Girl McKenna Dream Loft Bedroom. For just $225 you get a loft bed with ladder, a chair, faux accessories, a pillow for McKenna's pet Goldendoodle Cooper (sold separately) and — I could not make this stuff up — an "encouragement" mirror.

McKenna herself, of course, is also sold separately. But who could resist her? The catalog shows her in all her stylish cuteness, standing in her Dream Loft Bedroom with one leg in an ultra-fashionable cast and leaning on an adorable pair of crutches (cast and crutches sold separately – payment plans available).

I had to wonder: Did she break her leg falling

out of her Dream Loft?

I asked my friend if there was any chance the family would be adding McKenna's Dream Loft Bedroom to their existing home. Because she is fiscally responsible, she laughed and said that if she were going to spend several hundred bucks on a bed, her daughter had better be the one sleeping in it. And that she'd rather give her kids memorable experiences, like sledding with their cousins, than stuff.

I wanted to hug her.

Sure, we all like stuff. Especially new shiny stuff. But what are we telling children when we make waiting in line for stuff more important than anything else? When stores open their doors at 8 p.m. on Thanksgiving evening and families cut their celebrations short so they can go shopping? When people have literally been trampled, paralyzed and even killed at Black Friday sales? What stuff is worth that?

Ask McKenna. Maybe she'll let you borrow her American Girl Dream Ambulance and Riot Control Squad.

Last Updated April 2016
Source: http://blackfridaydeathcount.com/

Happy Birthday!

I just celebrated my Annual 29th Birthday, and though I had a great day complete with good friends, wine and mud pie, I'm starting to feel like maybe I need to step it up. While I agree with Dave Barry that the time to stop making a big deal about your birthday is age 11, I'm tempted to try something new and different next year. Judging from my friends' kids' birthday celebrations, traditional celebrations like bringing cupcakes to school just doesn't cut it anymore. (Besides, cupcakes now have to be vegan, peanut-free and gluten-free, and then they taste like dirt.)

Even sleepovers, which were great fun for me as a kid and not so much for my parents, have been replaced by elaborate, expensive productions. We used to play Ouija and hold séances. Now parents host tarot card parties and the kids get their astrological charts done. We used to braid each other's hair and paint our nails. Now the girls have a spa day at a local resort. We used to dance around to the Bay City Rollers and Shaun Cassidy. Now the birthday girl takes five of her friends in a limo to see Justin Bieber and meet him backstage. If it were legal, she might get to sleep with him.

There also is a whole new trend: Birthday parties designed for profit. My friend's daughter, Sara, recently attended a birthday party that turned out to be — I could not make this up — a Mary Kay demo. (By the way, Sara is 12.)

In retrospect, my friend says she should have known that something was not right when the birthday girl texted that morning that Sara should bring sodas to the party. And then texted again a bit later that she should bring cash, too.

Not only were the seventh-grade guests subjected to a day of pore-cleansing face masks and smoky eye make-up applications by a professional salesperson, the girl's mother also seized the opportunity to peddle her handmade jewelry. Both salesperson and hostess seemed perturbed when Sara, who doesn't wear makeup or elaborate jewelry, bought nothing. (Because she's 12.)

The goody bag contained a loofah and bath

products. Much to Sara's dismay, however, there were no anti-aging cream samples.

REPRODUCTIVE RIGHTS. AND WRONGS.

NO COMMENT

As you may have gathered from the title of this book, I don't have children. My family and friends seem to love me regardless. (By the way, *irregardless* is not a word, but that's another rant altogether and will be addressed along with *heighth* and *whole nother*.)

Anyway. So I am continually surprised by the inappropriate comments made to me and other childless women by people who don't know us well enough to discuss the weather, much less our reproductive status when they learn we don't have children. For example:

Oh, that's okay.

Um, yes, I'm aware of that. Thanks so much for your approval. How would it go over if I told you that you had too many children? Or not enough? A friend who has one son has repeatedly been told that only children are lonely, spoiled, miss out on important sibling relationships, and so on. Do these people consider that maybe a woman can't have more children? Or tried, and lost them? Or simply doesn't want any more? And that in any case, it's none of their business?

It's not too late. I know a woman who had a baby when she was [insert 45+ value].

How nice for her. And yes, I know about the woman in Europe who gave birth at age 57. (And I think that's crazy – but I would never tell her that, because it's her intensely personal decision and what I think doesn't matter in the least.) And anyway, why are you assuming that every woman wants children? Or hasn't already tried to have them?

Oh, you're going to regret that later.

I'll take my chances. What I already regret, however, is the time I've wasted having a conversation with someone so rude and condescending.

That's very selfish.

Yes, it is certainly very selfish to live your life the way you want versus the way other people expect you to. Especially when you are not hurting anyone in the process. But I'm thinking it's even more selfish to have kids you can't afford, don't have time for, expect other people to care for and/or raise, or just don't really want, because you thought you *should* have kids because all of your friends have kids. And who decides how many kids you need to have before you're no longer selfish?

How does your mother feel about that?

Shockingly, my mother feels I should live my own life and make my own decisions according to what makes me happy. Now is that selfish or what? The guilt is overwhelming.

But who is going to take care of you when you're old?

That one's easy. Three young, handsome, muscular Italian men will be cooking, cleaning, massaging my feet and bringing me fruity drinks with umbrellas in them along with my medications while I sit by my pool overlooking the ocean. I'll be paying for Guiseppe, Leonardo and Marco with all the money I've saved by not having kids.

Intervention

Yes, every once in a while I do have moments of longing for a child. Sometimes it's when I'm surfing and I see a dad teaching his young daughter to surf. Or when I see my friends' little ones laughing their heads off at a silly joke. Once in a while, I'll feel a twinge of regret.

Fortunately, I have friends with kids whom I can call when I have moments like this, and they bring me back to reality.

Case in point: I stopped in at a Starbucks during the holidays. It was a chilly, rainy morning, and inside the ambiance was warm and festive. Christmas carols played, lights twinkled, and a young mom and her two adorable toddler daughters were snuggled together in a booth, sharing cookies and hot chocolate.

I walked out and immediately called my good

friend and mom, Kathy.

"I'm having a 'maybe I should have had kids' moment," I confessed.

"Why?" she asked. "What happened?"

I told her about the happy family scene at Starbucks.

She scoffed. "Oh, this one is easy. Are you still there?"

"No, I left."

"Ok, turn around, go back in, and find a seat," she instructed. "Wait five minutes and you'll witness The Spill. That will be followed by The Crying, and then The Tantrum."

I immediately felt better. It's like having a sponsor.

I was taking care of her two young girls once while she ran a marathon. She had to be at the starting line at sunrise, and I asked what to do if the kids woke up to find her gone.

"They probably won't even wake up until I get back," she said, lacing up her shoes. "But if they do, just put one of the videos on and they'll be fine."

"Any one in particular?" I asked. "Ben & Jerry?"

She sighed. "It's Tom & Jerry. And that, right there, illustrates the difference between your life and mine."

The girls woke up minutes after she left. Ben &Tom & Jerry, I love all of you.

DOGMA

I recently read a blog by a woman who complained about how her childless friends with dogs constantly offered child-rearing advice based on their experiences as pet owners. (Now before I even get rolling, can I just say that she must have some odd friends? Who does that? When my friend complains that her child wet the bed again, it would never, ever occur to me to commiserate by telling her what I do when my cat misses the litterbox.)

Anyway. Her premise was that people with animals don't understand that there are major differences between raising children and raising pets. Really? Is there anyone with more than a speck of intelligence who thinks these responsibilities are interchangeable? She went on to list a number of things her daughter does that are, in her view, far more horrible than anything a dog could do. (Honestly, by the end of the article I got the feeling she intensely dislikes her daughter and wishes she had a dog instead, but that's just my take.)

But what I found even more fascinating than her point of view and her weird friends were the public comments that followed. They quickly turned into a vitriolic debate of children vs. pets, with each side becoming increasingly caustic about which is the better choice. The pet people accused parents of bringing ungrateful spoiled brats into the world and then acting superior about it, while the child people stated that pet people are selfish and that people who don't have children have no idea what love really is.

(And I have to stop right here and tell you how offensive this last statement is. I've heard it in various forms. "You don't know love until you have a child." So I assume those of us who don't have kids are just screwed as far as feeling real love? And women who are simply unable to have children — I guess they will never know what it is like to truly love someone? If you personally have never loved anyone as much as you love your child, fine. Say it that way. But don't define love for anyone else.)

Anyway. Is the country not divided enough

without having a debate over two legs vs. four? Why does one have to be the better choice? For that matter, why do people feel they have to defend their choice at all?

I have friends who have kids. I have friends who have dogs and/or cats. I have friends who have kids and dogs, and a couple of friends who have kids, dogs and cats. Most coexist beautifully. (Often, the animals coexist better than the kids.) Whether you care for a child or an animal, the important thing is that you *care*. Can we just leave it at that and stop arguing over who cares the most?

(Seriously though — buying baby outfits for the dog and pushing it in a stroller? That's a little messed up.)

No, I don't want to go to your dog's birthday party...freak.

My cat is getting married that weekend.

SAVING THE WORLD THROUGH STERILIZATION

And on the other side, we have the people who believe they are doing the world an enormous favor by not having children. Yes, I find it intrusive when people question my reproductive status, but I also find it extremely offensive when people who don't have kids suggest that they are better human beings because they're not contributing to overpopulation.

I was floored after reading the following comments on an environmental conservation website's discussion board:

"I did my share by remaining child-free. Having oneself sterilized without reproducing is a gift to Mother Earth."

"It's important to not add to the population. Besides, those who live rich, full, meaningful lives don't need children to fulfill them."

(No, I'm not making this up.)

It wasn't April Fools' Day or anything, although clearly several fools were present. I was stunned by the superiority and self-righteousness. (Not surprisingly, these are the people who insist on using the term "child-free.") More than one commenter responded that if these people felt so strongly about reducing the population, perhaps they should start with themselves.

Yes, having kids you can't or don't want to take care of is thoughtless and irresponsible. But having kids because you want to be a loving parent and raise responsible future adults? Apparently, you just hate the planet.

Parents Behaving Badly

Table Manners

When did "family-friendly" become a euphemism for "anything goes"?

I was having lunch with a few friends recently. Seated next to us were what appeared to be a mom, grandmother, and baby. The baby was really cute — until mom put her on the table halfway through their meal and let her crawl across it to grandma, who then seated Adorable Baby, diapers and all, square on the table and played with her. On the table. In a restaurant. That was *not* a

Chuck E. Cheese.

We watched with a mixture of fascination and revulsion to see if they might actually change the baby's diaper on the table while they were at it, but no. Perhaps they thought that would be inappropriate.

At this point, my friend Erika told us about the mom she'd seen who allowed her baby to suck on the salt shaker as if it were a bottle — and then simply put it back on the table when the kid lost interest. Note to self: Never salt anything in a restaurant again. In fact, all condiments that do not have a protective cap are off limits.

Maybe I'll just eat at home.

And while we're talking condiments...when your kid knocks one off of the table and it explodes all over the floor and makes a huge mess, that's (shockingly) not the restaurant's fault! Which is what I really wanted to tell the woman whose little girl (age somewhere between three and 12 — I never can tell) sent a syrup bottle flying off the table at breakfast last week. As she stood next to our table waiting for the busboy to clean it up, she sniped to her husband, "I don't know why they put glass bottles on the table." Of course! Blame the restaurant! In fact, why not just serve everything on paper plates with plastic utensils and paper cups? Or even better — sippy cups for all!

Kids are kids, and we've all spilled stuff. I still do. Accidents happen. It's no reflection on you — until you refuse to take even a shred of responsibility and start assigning blame.

If your kid makes a mess, acknowledge it. Maybe even help clean it up. Years ago, I was at breakfast (yes, as a matter of fact I do eat out a lot) with friends who both had young kids. They didn't seat the kids on the table or even allow them to gnaw on the condiment bottles. They left a generous tip because it's an undisputed fact that kids are messy. And when my friend's toddler started hurling his mini-pancakes into the air like Frisbees as we were preparing to leave, she immediately stopped him, picked up the pieces and started peeling off dollar bills to add to the tip pile.

(Although I don't know why she felt the need to leave a tip in the first place. If the stupid restaurant didn't serve Frisbee-shaped food, these things wouldn't happen.)

Darla Neugebauer, the owner of Marcy's Diner in Portland, Maine, may have lost some customers when she snapped at a crying child. But she also may have gained some. According to Darla, the girl's parents ordered pancakes for their daughter but didn't feed them to her, and ignored her subsequent cries. Darla asked the family to finish their meal, or take the wailing girl outside, to no avail. Finally, she slammed her hands on the counter and told the girl to be quiet. The crying ceased, but the mother was just getting started. She posted on the diner's Facebook page about the experience, and people vowed never to eat there again.

Darla admits she may have used poor judgement, but she says, "Life's full of choices and you've got to live with all of them. I chose to yell at a kid, it made her shut-up, which made me happy, it made my staff happy, it made the 75 other people

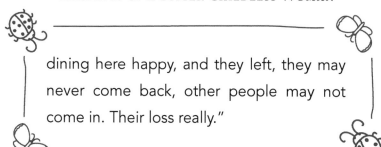

dining here happy, and they left, they may never come back, other people may not come in. Their loss really."

DOG EARS

You know that unbelievably ear-splitting, high-pitched squeal that only babies and Mariah Carey are capable of emitting? I'm convinced that it is audible solely to dogs and people without children. I'm also convinced that babies are capable of emitting it only in fine restaurants and small, quiet, enclosed areas.

Case in point: My sister and I took my mom to dinner on a Saturday night at an upscale Italian restaurant. The guests were almost exclusively adults — except for the table (of course) nearest to us. No sooner had we opened our menus than the first shrill screech pierced the air. I fully expected my wine glass to shatter.

We looked over expecting to see a large bird being tortured, but saw only an infant sitting in the lap of its (sex was indeterminate) completely oblivious mother, who simply raised her voice to continue her conversation above the din. Even a second shriek failed to elicit more than a distracted pat on the baby's back while mom used her other hand to refill her wine, and continued her chatter without missing a beat. Never mind that the other parties in the cozy room had stopped eating and turned to stare at the baby, presumably to ensure it wasn't on fire.

Another time, I was out for coffee with a very good friend and her two-year-old daughter, who had been asleep in the car but was (of course) wide awake once we arrived at the coffee shop. She proceeded to run around the shop like a whirling dervish, screaming her head off, while other patrons shot us dirty looks. When I offered to go get her, my friend looked up from her bagel and nonchalantly asked, "Why? Is she being loud?"

Of course, this behavior is perfectly acceptable in the right places. I was catching up with a friend at McDonald's while her kids ran rampant through the outdoor Playland, shrieking like banshees, and she turned to me and said, "Oh no, you're going to put me in a rant, aren't you?" No, because we're at McDonald's Playland and your kids are behaving normally. (I think she was secretly disappointed.) If we had met at a pricey steakhouse, she might have made the cut.

Anyway. I can only conclude that when humans reproduce, their auditory processing abilities become compromised and they can no longer hear tones that exceed a certain pitch. I simply cannot believe that anyone who can hear that preternatural squeal would assume that it isn't, to put it mildly, just a bit disruptive. Another friend explained, "That's just what babies do. You can't help it."

Actually, you can. There's a simple solution. When I was growing up Catholic, we had a "crying room" in church, an enclosed room where parents sat with their screaming kids so as not to disrupt the priest or distract the choir. I'd like to propose a crying room for nice restaurants — two or three tables in a soundproofed room where parents who insist on bringing screeching babies to a fine dining establishment can let them shriek to their hearts' content. And those of us who are paying a lot of money for a pleasant, relaxing dining experience can have one. And dogs aren't circling outside the door.

FAMILY-FRIENDLY DINING? NOT SO MUCH.

In 2011, a Monterey, California restaurant banned strollers, high chairs, booster seats and crying or loud children.

A sign in the restaurant says, "No strollers. No high chairs. No booster chairs. Children crying or making loud noises are a distraction to other diners, and as such are not allowed in the dining room."

Many parents did not take the news well. "I think it's ridiculous," said one visitor. "I think kids need to know how to behave in restaurants, and if you don't take them to them, they don't know how to behave and they shouldn't be kept hidden away, so I think it's ridiculous. Kids should be allowed in restaurants." [*Editor's note: See "Let's Pretend" rant on page 10. And I'm not sure real-life experience is going to help a kid in a high chair learn how to behave in a restaurant.*]

Well-behaved children (and parents) are still welcome at the restaurant, and owner Chris Shake doesn't believe the new rules will hurt business.

"Let's put it this way, I haven't had a down year for over 20 years," Shake said. "Our business continues to grow."

ALLERGY SEASON

After spending a fun and amusing morning at a wildlife park with my good friend Christine and her two young kids (and learning more about porcupine mating habits than I ever wanted to know), mom asked where the kids wanted to go for lunch. The response was immediate and unanimous: "McDonald's!!!"

Christine strongly prefers that her kids avoid McDonald's (because she strongly prefers that they consume meals from food groups other than fat, sodium and high-fructose corn syrup.) And the kids strongly preferred to go. So after her numerous suggestions of other tasty alternatives were repeatedly drowned out by begging and pleading, Christine finally announced, "We can't go to McDonald's. Aunt Jeanne's allergic."

The cacophony came to an abrupt halt and was replaced by stunned silence. Horrified, little John turned to me and asked, "You ARE?" Clearly a fate worse than death. Both kids backed away, presumably in case I might be contagious.

I admit that I, too, was a bit surprised to learn that I was allergic to McDonald's. But I quickly played along. "Yes, I am," I said solemnly, then covertly shot Christine a "WTF?" look.

Actually, I was fine with this. I rarely go to McDonald's except for the occasional drive-thru ice cream cone, so it's not like I'm going to be strolling into their house with a bag full of McNuggets anytime soon. If she had said I was allergic to pizza, we'd have a problem.

I can only imagine how frustrating it must be to have constant pleading and whining, and no amount of "Because I said so" makes a dent. I actually thought the explanation that I was allergic to McDonald's was pretty fast thinking. In fact, allergies seem to have become the new "out" for parents – and an apparently acceptable lie to tell their children. I have friends who have refused their kids' requests for dogs, cats and birds because "Dad's allergic." (He's not.)

But I'm surprised there's not more of a backlash

about lying to kids, especially in our "I don't let my children believe in Santa Claus because it sets them up for a crushing disappointment" society. What's going to happen in 10 years when I get a hankering for a cheap ice cream cone and now-teenage John is working the drive-thru window? When the kids figure out that their parents have been coming to my cat-friendly house for years and dad never once needed an EpiPen®? As a non-parent, I'm curious about where parents draw the line.

But more so, I'm grateful. I have the perfect new "out" for anything I don't want to do. Cornered to buy Girl Scout cookies? Sorry, allergic. Invited to a four-year-old's birthday party at Chuck E. Cheese? Wish I could. Deadly allergies.

And perhaps best of all: "So why don't you have kids?" I'll smile sadly and say, "I would, but I'm allergic."

VELCRO CHILDREN

As a childless woman, there's a lot I don't know about kids. However, I do know that at birth, the child is connected to the mother via the umbilical cord. This cord is then cut, allowing mother and baby to function as wholly independent beings.

It's that last part that I think some parents don't quite get.

What is it with parents who refuse to go anywhere without their children? And get very offended at the suggestion that perhaps it is inappropriate to bring said children to a special event, like a wedding or dinner party or — and of course I'm speaking purely hypothetically here — a girls' night out with friends you haven't seen in a long time?

For example (purely hypothetical, remember),

say four of us get together for drinks, eager to let loose with some hardcore "girl talk" about our significant others, menstrual cycles, sex lives, and so on. We're just getting rolling when "Jane" shows up with her two daughters. Her two very young daughters. The girl chat, R-rated language and unedited subject matter come to a screeching halt. The girls become the center of mom's attention and, by default, everyone else's as well. When one friend asked if Jane had trouble getting a sitter, Jane said no — she just thought it would be fun for the girls to come along.

Um, fun for whom? The other women who had arranged childcare for their kids in eager anticipation of some unrestricted girl time?

One couple declined a black-tie New Year's Eve adult-only house party invitation because the baby wasn't invited. Their verbatim response? "I'm sorry, but we're a family now, and if our child isn't included then we can't make it either." Sheesh – even the hosts arranged for their own kid to spend the night with a friend!

I understand that sometimes parents have to bring the kids to an adults-only event. Sitters fall through or unexpected conflicts arise, and we'd rather see you with your kids than not see you at all. But we're hoping they won't be inextricably attached to you all night. When "Sue" and "Bob" had to bring "Josh" to a friend's small dinner party, Josh and mom were inseparable. Before dinner, she carried him around while she mingled, including him in conversation (he's four). During dinner, Josh sat on her lap while she ate, at one point taking a break from sucking on his ratty stuffed dinosaur to hurl the soggy mess across the dinner table in a one-sided game of catch. After dinner, he insisted that daddy play "dump truck" with him. If you're not familiar with this game, picture a trash collection vehicle (Josh's dad) picking up the dumpster (Josh), inverting it and shaking its contents into the bin. Josh screamed with laughter, and then vomited all over the coffee table.

My friend hasn't had a dinner party since.

It Takes a Village of Idiots

Hang Up and Parent

You know how people claim that cats can tell when someone doesn't particularly want them around, and as a result they instantly and inextricably Velcro themselves to that person? It's like that with me and kids.

Most of the kids I seem to attract have parents who apparently can't be bothered with them. As a result, they flock to the nearest available adult who seems even remotely unoccupied (that would be me).

Case in point: One afternoon I was on the beach, attempting to relax on my ridiculously oversized beach towel, sipping a ridiculously overpriced latte, and enjoying having an hour to read. At one point I looked up and waved at a little girl nearby.

Rookie mistake.

Brandishing a plastic bucket and tiny shovel, she brazenly invaded the personal space of which I am fiercely overprotective and asked if I would help her build a sand city. Not just a castle — a city. It's heartwarming to see kids with ambition.

"Where's your mom?"

Because maybe this kid is lost. Certainly her parents wouldn't turn her loose to pester the nice lady trying to read, right? Or more importantly, want their child engaging random strangers in conversation and activity at a public beach?

Future urban renewal developer points to a woman sitting not ten feet away from us, chatting on her phone.

"Why don't you ask her to help you?"

"She's on the phone."

Of course she is.

In a coffee shop, an adorable kid took refuge under our table in an attempt to lure mom away from her laptop and engage her in hide and seek.

On a cross-country flight, my five-year-old middle-seat neighbor, ostensibly a CIA agent in training, relentlessly interrogated me about my family, their names, their pets, and their houses while her mom was busy watching the movie. (Airlines, take note: Collude with TSA to prohibit passengers from bringing DVD players and handheld games on board, and then rent them in-flight to parents. You'd make a fortune, and we could all go back to checking bags for free.)

I'm all in favor of playdates with my friends' kids. I can draw in 3D sidewalk chalk, fall off of a skateboard and read *Where the Wild Things Are* with the best of them. I love it when my niece unintentionally (I hope) creates a horrifying caricature of me in purple glitter crayon. Or when my attempts at imitating barn animals are met with hysterical laughter. But when anonymous kids seek the attention of strangers, it's usually because their parents are too busy to notice.

NOT NOW HONEY, I'M ON THE PHONE

A 2014 study published in the journal Pediatrics found that when parents use their mobile devices, they often ignore their children.

Boston Medical Center researchers observed parent-child interactions at fast food restaurants while parents were on their smartphones or mobile tablets. Of the 55 families observed, 40 were engrossed in their mobile devices. Close to 75 percent used their device at least once during the meal, and nearly a third used them during the entire meal.

How did the kids react? Some entertained themselves, while others acted out. According to the study, highly absorbed caregivers often responded harshly to child misbehavior. One child who tried to lift his mother's head up from the device had his hands shoved away.

Dr. Jenny S. Radesky, lead author of the study, doesn't believe parents should completely abandon their phones. But she says it does raise the issue that parents need to create boundaries for mobile devices when they are with their children.

Everyone Gets a Trophy!

When I was 9 or 10, I played tee-ball through my neighborhood park district. This was my first foray into group sports outside of gym class. (Where, by the way, I was inevitably one of the last picked for any team, and never, ever selected as team captain. This has not scarred me for life. Not at all.)

Anyway. So I was a horrible tee-ball player. A good day was when I didn't make the last strike-out of the game. (I know, how does one strike out in tee-ball? The ball isn't even in motion!) I somehow persevered through the season though, and at the end of the summer I received a trophy! I was named "Most Improved" by my coach and teammates. In other words, I REALLY sucked at the start, and by the end I sucked less! What a dubious honor!

To this day, I think I would have felt better about getting no award at all.

Decades later, this embarrassingly uncomfortable attempt to give every child props regardless of performance has now become everyday practice, as evidenced by the ubiquitous bumper stickers on almost every parent's car:

"My Child was Student of the Month at Country Day."

"I Have an Honor Student at Dewey Academy."

"My Son was Named a Good Citizen at St. Martha's Elementary."

There is a bumper sticker accolade for everything, and certainly many are well-deserved. But, alas, not everyone can be a Student of the Month, an Honor Student or even a Good Citizen. And for the unfortunate rest, we have the bumper sticker on the car in front of me last week:

"My Child was Recognized at Alta Middle School."

You child was *recognized*? As what? The kid who was spraying graffiti on the gym walls? The newest mug shot on the FBI Most Wanted List?

Or did someone at school simply identify him? "Hey, isn't that kid in Mrs. Stewart's class?" "Yes, he is. Give his mom a bumper sticker."

I have a new business idea: Bumper stickers for the underachiever.

"My Child Goes to School."

Order yours early, these coveted commendations are going to sell out fast.

Too Old to Matter

ere in sunny Southern California, we have it all — beautiful beaches, majestic mountains, perfect climate, random freeway shootings. (Hey, I didn't say it was all good.) So, about that last one...a few days ago, a 21-year-old college student was driving to school around 7:30 a.m. and started having trouble breathing. Eventually, she realized she'd been shot, apparently by a random gunman on the freeway. Another driver discovered a bullet hole in his rear window frame.

I read the story online and then, because I like to stress myself out, read the public comments. (Which is depressing in itself because, regardless of the sentiment, a good 85 percent of those who post comments cannot differentiate between your/you're, there/their or to/too. Or spell their way out of first grade. Or grasp Basic rules Of capitalization. As a writer, I find this distressing. But that's another rant.)

Anyway. Back to the sentiment. I didn't have to read much before I encountered the inevitable: "What were they thinking? There could have been a child in that car!"

Really? REALLY? Isn't the random shooting of an innocent person on the freeway bad enough? Why would it be worse if it had been a child? There also could have been a teenager, a middle-aged dad or an elderly parent in the car. To their friends and family, it's pretty awful — even if they're adults and, apparently, not as important as children. (And call me a cynic, but I doubt anyone evil enough to commit this crime was thinking, "Wait, maybe firing randomly into rush hour traffic is a bad idea — I might hit a child.")

As a friend pointed out, it's like the Baby on Board signs that were unavoidable a while back. "Please smash into someone else's car. I've got an infant here."

Or the California Transportation Department ads urging drivers to watch out for road crews on the freeway because "remember, they could be someone's mom or dad." But if you're sure the worker in the orange vest has no kids, drive as recklessly as you'd like. In fact, just plow into the group.

Or the radio caller who expressed outrage that a fan of the rival team had been brutally beaten into a coma at a major league baseball game and angrily stated, "There are children at those games!" Right, because it's ok to pummel someone nearly to death as long as everyone present is over age 13.

And for that matter, what's the cutoff? Is it more tragic if the child is under age 14? 10? 7? At what age do we start to become inconsequential? Is there some Wally World-type cartoon-character sign somewhere that says: "Sorry! You must be shorter than this sign to matter."

Of course it is tragic when an innocent child is killed. But it is also tragic when it happens to an innocent teenager, a college student, an adult in his prime or an elderly person — any of whom is likely someone's child, parent, sibling or best friend.

WRONG IS THE NEW RIGHT

My friend Mary, mother of four school-age kids, e-mailed me with this request: "Someone needs to do a rant about the BS terms school administrators use. Try to decipher this garbage from their middle school's website regarding some online testing they do."

So here we go.

When I first read the paragraph she sent, I assumed she had copied it incorrectly because it sounded like gibberish. But no, it was correct:

"Acuity replaced Tungsten as our formative assessment for teachers when the State Board of Education replaced the Learning Standards with the Common Core Standards. Acuity measures those Common Core Standards. Acuity is a computer-based solution which enables teachers to accurately target instruction to the Common Core Standards in reading and mathematics. The Common Core Standards will soon be measured by the ISAT which is administered yearly in grades 3-8."

Mary noted that parents are encouraged to click on a link for additional information, where she encountered terminology including readiness, predictive, formative and summative assessment. She also learned that her children will be evaluated via a Learning Target Check. Formerly known as a "test."

To quote Mary, "You need a frigging thesaurus to see what it is your kids are getting graded on."

To quote Wikipedia: "Summative assessment (or summative evaluation) refers to the assessment of participants, and summarizes their development at a particular time. In contrast to formative assessment, the focus is on the outcome of a program. Summative assessment is characterized as assessment of learning and is contrasted with formative assessment, which is assessment for learning. This is taught in many educational programs in the United States.[citation needed] Scriven claims that while all assessment technique can be summative, only some are formative."

To quote Mary: "Who the hell is Scriven? Am I supposed to know? I tell you, it's a minefield."

And let's not get started on Common Core. Apparently, the goal in math is no longer to get the right answer. Instead, the goal is to justify how you got the wrong answer. And if your explanation makes sense, you've succeeded.

As my civil engineer boyfriend pointed out, if you get the wrong answer in math — even if you have a brilliant explanation of how you got there — the bridge collapses and everyone dies.

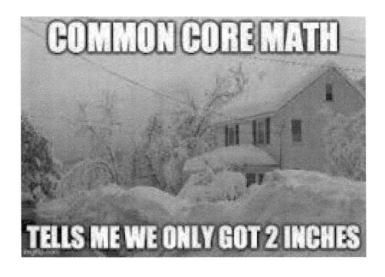

COMMON CORE MATH
TELLS ME WE ONLY GOT 2 INCHES

School's Out

When I was in school, in addition to having to walk five miles in the snow uphill both ways, we eagerly anticipated the last day of the school year. We cleaned out our desks, collected our report cards, and when the final bell rang, we were out of there like human cannonballs. And we didn't think about school again until September.

(And here I must digress. Yes, it was a long time ago, but our school year ended the week before Memorial Day, and we went back the Tuesday after Labor Day. Every year. It was logical. It was predictable. Our parents could plan vacations and summer activities. Now, it's all over the map. Some kids get out early May. Some get out late June. Some get out late June and go back early August, but have two weeks off in October and a random week in February, and then spring break, which no longer has anything to do with spring. When you're a parent with two or more kids on different school schedules, how do you plan anything?)

Anyway. Apparently a definitive end to the school year is a thing of the past. According to my parent friends, the end of the school year is now marked by a series of events that begins about two weeks prior to the official last day. These may include, and this is by no means a complete list: The Perfect Attendance Pancake Breakfast, The School Movie and Pajama Night, The End-of-the-Year Family Picnic, The Teacher Appreciation Lunch, and numerous events for school sports, clubs and activity groups. There is probably an End-of-the-Year Detention in the principal's office, unless it is canceled because the principal has to attend the Principal's Year-End Tea with the honor students.

And then there is graduation. I graduated from eighth grade, high school, and college. So far, my friend's son has graduated from preschool, kindergarten, first grade, fifth grade, junior high and high school. Each of these, naturally, requires family to be in attendance (and therefore take time off of work) and some kind of party with gifts.

Preschool graduation? Is there a valedictorian?

"As we move forward with our young lives, I know we will accomplish great things. Riding a bicycle without training wheels. Sleeping without a nightlight. Go forth into the world, but don't cross the street."

And then he goes down for his nap.

It's for the Children

Recently, while leaving the grocery store, I was accosted by two women raising funds for the local library. A little backstory: First of all, I already support the local library. It's called "taxes." Second, let me just mention that our library was renovated several years ago, and is now nicer than many luxury hotels. It has a sweeping ocean view, outside decks with patio furniture and lounge chairs, comfy couches inside, a gourmet coffee cart, free Wi-Fi, electronic self-checkout that is far superior to anything at the grocery store, and free Internet stations generally occupied most of the day by local beach bums — I'm sorry, "transients"— many of whom who would greatly benefit from a bar of soap and a comb. (I'm not being callous. Some of these guys will proudly tell you that "beach dweller" is their lifestyle choice.)

Anyway. So, because our library is actually doing quite well and I'm doing my part as a tax-paying citizen who frequently donates used books, I politely declined. One woman then said, "Your donation helps support the entire community." Yes, I'm sure it does. Especially the transient demographic. (And it's not like they're seeking respite from the bitter cold. This is Southern California.)

I began to walk away and the other woman called out after me, "It's for the children!"

Wait. Hold everything! *It's for the children??* Why didn't you say that first? Here's a blank check! And here, take my jewelry, too.

Why should the idea that "it's for the children" instantly mandate financial support? It's like a last-ditch effort to shame us into donating no matter what the cause: libraries, skate parks, carpool lanes, yet another Starbucks, whatever.

(And in this case, it's hardly "for the children." Children in this town have no need to use the library; they're downloading books and researching projects on the iPads provided by the schools.)

I'm certainly not against fundraising. I've donated to MADD: Mothers Against Drunk Driving (which, incidentally, my mother consistently refers to as Mad Mothers Against Driving). I support several charitable organizations, including wildlife preservation, clean oceans, cancer prevention and animal rescue. I also support the right to run errands in peace without being guilted into donating — whether it is for the children, the humpback whale or anyone else.

I think I'll start standing outside the grocery store with a petition to raise funds for a ban on fundraising petitions at grocery stores. I hope you will support me. It's for the children.

GUESS WHAT?

I t was a Saturday, late afternoon, at Trader Joe's. Sunday was a big TV football day, and the place was really crowded. My boyfriend was deftly navigating our cart through the throngs of shoppers when a little boy on skate shoes suddenly darted across the aisle and nearly crashed head-first into the sharp plastic corner of the cart. My boyfriend, a civil engineer whose goal in every situation is to keep the flow of traffic moving as efficiently and safely as possible, quickly swerved to miss him and muttered a curse.

Let me point out that he didn't yell at the kid. He just said a garden-variety, PG-rated expletive, mostly under his breath. The kid didn't hear it, and since his parents were nowhere to be found, neither did they.

But a woman standing next to us – unrelated to

all parties – apparently did. She gave us her Most Condescending Smile and sneered, "I'm guessing you don't have children." Then she walked away.

We stood there in stunned silence for a second, which in retrospect was probably a good thing.

Hey, lady? I'm guessing that if we did have children, especially young and very energetic children, they wouldn't be roller skating completely unsupervised through the narrow aisles of a busy grocery store. And I'm guessing you're one of those moms whose children can do no wrong, and it's always the other child's fault. And finally, I'm guessing you would be shocked if you knew we were shopping for snacks to bring to a child's birthday celebration that evening, because we're not ogres and we actually do like children, but we think it might be a good idea not to let them skate through a crowded store, because we'd rather not see anybody lose an eye on the corner of a shopping cart. And because this is California, file a lawsuit against us, the store, the manufacturer of the cart and the skates, and the city.

But, I'm just guessing.

Elsewhere in the Village

Do Si Don'ts

"We're selling Girl Scout cookies!"

Apparently. That would explain why I almost have to pole vault over your display table to make my way into the store.

Really, I like Girl Scouts. I was a Brownie. For a couple of weeks. It's a long story.

So I make eye contact, I smile…and here we go.

No, thank you, I already bought some.

Yes, I bought some for the troops too.

No, I don't want "just one more box." Even if

you are competing to sell more than anyone else in your troop. (You are familiar with the economic meltdown in this country, correct? Do they still cover current events in school?)

Yes, I'm sure. And I'm not going to change my mind while I'm in the store, so there's no need for you to accost me again on the way out. Or for your mom to give me the evil eye.

Naptime

I started working from home about 10 years ago after my then-employer "reorganized" for the third time in 18 months and eliminated my position. (A fact I learned when a guy wearing a tool belt walked into my freestanding office without warning and began dismantling it while I was sitting at my desk. Seriously.)

Anyway, one afternoon, perhaps exhausted by the daily commute from my bedroom to my living room, I found myself yawning in front of my computer and thinking, "I really wish I could take a nap."

Then I realized: I can. And I did. And a decade later, I still do.

And when I mention this to people, especially people who are employed outside the home, you'd think I'm a complete slacker.

"You *nap?*" Utter disbelief. "During the *day?*" (Yes. When I nap at night, it's called "sleeping.")

"My daughter stopped napping when she was five," one of my mom friends disdainfully informed me.

Well, there's the problem. Why do we stop napping once we're grown-ups? As adults, we're getting less sleep than we did as children, our lives are probably much more stressful than theirs, and I think it's safe to say we do a lot more during the day than four-year-olds. Sometimes, when 3 p.m. rolls around, I can barely keep my eyes open. On these days, napping isn't an option, it's a requirement. I crash out for 45 minutes, and I usually sleep better than I ever do at night.

In fact, I've woken up from naps not knowing where I was. Or when I went to sleep. Once, shortly after the end of daylight savings time, I woke up so disoriented that I made coffee, fed my cats and took a shower. It was only after I got out of the shower and freaked out because it was not getting lighter outside that I remembered I'd been napping, and it was early evening, not early morning.

Scientific research has proven that a short nap in the afternoon can be energizing and make you far more productive. So there! Adult napping is healthy. It makes me more valuable to my clients (but they don't need to know my 3 p.m. meeting is with my pillow.) I'm less cranky, and I eat all my dinner.

Now if I can just get the kids at the pool to be quiet. Don't they realize some of us nap, I mean work, at home?

Love Me on Facebook

I got sucked into the Facebook vortex by playing Scrabble, and sometimes I spend more time than I would like to admit reading about the comings and goings of my family, friends and people who automatically add anyone they have ever met, or never met, to their four-figure friends list.

I like seeing people's vacation photos, hearing about new jobs and exciting events, keeping up with friends who live across the country and seeing photos of what they're having for dinner. And yes, I even enjoy posts about their kids and, of course, their pets. But the posts that never fail to get my eyes rolling are the saccharine, ultra-gushing, look-how-happy-we-are messages ostensibly meant purely for someone's spouse — who is presumably right there in the same house, if not the same room

— yet plastered for the world to see:

"Happy Mother's Day to my amazing wife Elizabeth who is a perfect mother to our beautiful teenage daughter Madison." (In case your amazing wife Elizabeth, as opposed to your other wives, didn't know which teenage daughter you were referring to?)

"Happy birthday to my gorgeous and sexy husband! I can't wait to celebrate with you tonight! ;-) " (How about emailing or sexting him instead? Please? The rest of us don't need to be apprised of your impending intimacy. And now I can't unsee this.)

I recently learned that some people apparently expect this public coronation from their partners. I personally know a woman whose husband did not speak to her for a full day after she failed to post birthday greetings on his Facebook page. Never mind that they celebrated in person with their kids — he wanted the public glory.

(I also know of a woman who publicly shamed her husband on Christmas morning for leaving her empty-handed after they had agreed not to exchange gifts. She posted: "Would someone please tell my husband that deciding not to exchange gifts doesn't mean he shouldn't get me *anything*?"

To which another friend replied: "I think you just did." I wonder if they are still married.)

Anyway. A thoughtful, heartfelt sentence or two flattering your husband/wife and announcing a special day is one thing. ("Happy to be celebrating 15 years with this guy!" and a photo of the couple is sweet, not saccharine.) Everyone appreciates a compliment. But some of these grandiose, over-the-top postings are a bit suspect. "See how much I love him/her? We have an awesome marriage. No, we do. We do! Really! That's why I'm posting this very personal message for all 859 of our Facebook friends to see."

And now let's go see who's unfriended me.

Acknowledgements

I would like to thank all of my friends with and without kids who shared their stories and thoughts with me — especially Mary, Kay, Tina and Joe. Thanks also to all who read some of these rants on my blog and reassured me that I am not alone and am far from bitter (especially the moms who agreed with me!).

And finally, a very heartfelt thanks to my own awesome mom who has always encouraged me to follow my heart (and never made me feel bad about not giving her grandchildren). If I'd had kids, Mom, I hope I would have been even half the amazing mother you are.

JEANNE BELLEZZO

Made in the USA
Monee, IL
30 November 2022

19067768R00070